I0417688

PULLED BY HORSES

A Memoir of Metfield, Suffolk in the 1930s

Evelyn Whiting

Copyright © 2011 Evelyn Whiting
All rights reserved.
ISBN: 1466213248
ISBN-13: 978-1466213241
Also available as an ebook from online retailers.

VILLAGE SHOPS

The village as I first knew it was very different from what it is today.

There were many shops in those days. The most important was Squire's general stores in the centre of the village on the green. Squire's was an intriguing place to visit, and sold just about everything. One side was grocery and provisions; here Annie Warne served customers and took orders, which were later delivered by pony cart. The pony was often tethered to the sheds, opposite Elmore Cottage. The other side of the shop sold the dry goods: clothes for all ages, shoes, hobnail boots that hung from the ceiling, bed linen, material for curtains, all kinds of hardware, paraffin, hats for ladies and gents, knitting wool and cottons. There was so much stock, you could hardly find room to stand to get served, probably hitting your head on all the wares hanging from above. There was always a long wait but no one seemed to mind; there was so much to see and always something to chat about. On dull days, hanging paraffin lamps were lit and I can remember the lovely smell and atmosphere of the place.

The Squire family had been licensees of the Red Lion public house – now the Red House – before it closed. They then moved into the shop. The sons had left home by then, and father had died. There was mother, Old Mary, and the daughters Miss Dinah and Miss Laura. In their youth, the girls were very naughty, shocking the neighbours by going out at night on an ancient motorbike and coming home at all hours. However, they remained unmarried. When I re-member them, Miss Dinah was a very sweet, gentle lady with time for everyone, and always loved the children, while Miss Laura was eccentric and vague. Both always seemed to wear knitted two-piece suits and were never seen without their tammies.

Miss Dinah died first and sadly the shop closed. Miss Laura lived to a good old age, although she lost her eye-sight. She was joined in the house by her cousin, Mrs Eva Fance, who had been widowed since the First World War. They were always arguing over food, each thinking the oth-er was having more than her share. Rats and mice roamed the house; once Eva Fance had made a meat pie and during the night the crust was eaten by vermin, so she made more pastry, baked it, and the pie was enjoyed for lunch.

The Squires owned many of the cottages in the vil-lage, buying them up when they were very cheap. What is now the front part of Metfield's only shop was built by one of the Squire sons, who was hoping to take trade away from the family. It proved to be a costly failure and soon closed, remaining that way for many years. William, another son, had gone to Canada to work in the lumber trade. He mar-ried there, returned to Metfield and bought the Firs. He had two daughters: Laura, later to be Mrs Tom Godbold, moth-er of Terry and Edith, who is still with us.

The other big shop, which was also the Post Office, was at the top of the Street. It was owned first by Mr and Mrs Hadingham, and then bought by Mr and Mrs Jack Pretty. This last couple ran a flourishing little business, Mrs Pretty doing the Post Office side of it. They retired in the early 1960s and moved into a new bungalow, which they named Elmside.

Just before this, the new back extension was added to today's general store, which opened to include the Post Office.

In my childhood, my pennies were spent at Mr Clutterham's sweet shop, now the Red House. He sold cigarettes and tobacco, and food items. The rows of jars of sweets and the chocolate novelties of those days were very tempting, and it was difficult to choose. Mr Clutterham was a dear old man, with snow-white hair and moustache, rather stout in build and always wearing a fawn warehouse coat. I used to run from the top of the lane, where the Ling brothers were working, two or three times a day to get Roger a twopenny Woodbine (five for 2d). He would not buy ten cigarettes at a time, though he usually gave me the odd penny change.

Then there was Percy and Faith Savage's shop, next to the Firs. They sold mainly fish and greengrocery, but also many other items. Percy had a van, with which he did a regular round of the surrounding villages, after he returned from war service.

Rusted's butcher's shop was at Doctor's Lodge and had been a family business for many years. The stables and coach house are now a separate flat. During the war, Hedley Rusted had a lovely horse called Blitz, which he drove before a cart, twice a week, to Stradbroke to fetch his meat quota. Mrs Ellen Rusted was a dear lady, always willing to help anyone; she taught many children at the Methodist Chapel Sunday School.

There was another pork butcher's shop at the end of Elmore Cottage. Mr James Parke rented it before 1939, and the animals were killed in the end shed.

LOCAL BUSINESSES

Teddy Poppy had his shoemaker's shed next to the Chapel and made a living there mending the villagers' boots and shoes. The place became a meeting place in the evenings for the men, who gathered there to exchange news.

On the corner at the top of Mill Lane stood Ikey Ling's harness-making shop – quite a large wooden one-storey building. Ikey, who lived in one end of Pond Cottage, was a bachelor, and was kept very busy making and mending harnesses for the many horses kept on the farms. After he died, the building was taken over by Harold Edgecombe, who used it for spraying cars. When the road was widened, it was demolished.

Before my time, there was a wheelwright's business in what is now Pear Tree Cottage, and another at the top of the Street. Also at Hillside an undertaker was installed. He also did metalwork, employing several men. As can be imagined, almost all the men of the village found work nearby.

There were two main building businesses. The Rusted brothers, Kenneth and Maurice, had their yard where Harmony now stands. Kenneth resided at the Gables next door, with his mother. They employed several men.

Elmore and Davy's premises were at the old Mill Yard, just inside the land, on the site of an old windmill. They specialised in repairing churches and old houses, also building new ones, providing work for many.

The Forge was also working. Ambrose Clutterham Junior (Honey) was the blacksmith, who did a good trade shoeing horses and repairing farm machinery, kitchen pots and so on.

After the closure of the Red Lion, there were still two pubs in Metfield. The Huntsman & Hounds was the main one, and very popular. The place was always full of locals and, during the war, perhaps rather too many servicemen. First there were the RAF; then came the Americans, who were stationed on the airfield, just up the road. Beer was sometimes in very short supply. The old Duke William was open then and was a very small old-fashioned pub with one room and a serving place. The Duke was run by a lady called Lib Riches, assisted by Charlie Barley; two lovely people. Then when the new Duke was built in the 1950s, they took over the tenancy. Sadly, in 1976, the Huntsman was closed and sold as a private house.

Three windmills were in use at one time, the one at Mill Lane, one up at the Coles place, and the other at Office Farm.

Metfield School was very well attended, with three teachers, the headmistress residing at Church Cottage. Sadly, about 1964, it had to close as the numbers of children fell. It was then bought by Mr Haxby and turned over to the pottery.

WORKING THE LAND

About five farms and several cottages were demolished to make way for the airfield, including Tithe Farm and Haggars. After the war, all these were amalgamated into surrounding land. The farms were the Willows, Metfield Hall, Nut Tree Farm, Hatten's, Grove Farm, Oak Hill, Villa Farm, Turkey Hall, Rookery Farm, Clarkes, Home Farm, Buttons and Valley Farm.

The Wilderness, Whitings, Mrs Watts Farm, Vale Farm, Office Farm, Town Farm, Street Farm, Rose Farm, and other smallholdings. As all work was done with horses, one can imagine how a living was made by all the different tradesmen, and how many men were needed to work the land.

At harvest time, for example, every field was mown round first by men with scythes to make a path for the binder. This corn was gathered up and tied by hand, using wisps of straw, to make sheaves. Then came the binder pulled by two horses, the tied sheaves falling at the side. Men came behind and made 'shocks' with six or eight sheaves. These were left to dry; oats took longer.

Then came the horse-drawn wagons: every sheaf was pitched by hand on to the wagon where another man loaded. My favourite job was riding the horse along the rows, stopping and starting at the shocks. Sometimes I was allowed to load, but I didn't like this job when we were barley carting. The loaded wagons were then taken to the stackyard, where more men unloaded and stacked, one on the wagon, one in the 'bully hole' and one on top. The stacks themselves were a work of art. Every sheaf had to be placed exactly right, or they would slip and disaster would occur. The men took pleasure in walking round on Sunday mornings to view each other's work and to criticise. The stacks were then neatly thatched to keep out the rain.

After harvest the fields were mucked. This was all dug from the buildings by a four-tined fork, loaded onto tumbrels and carted to the fields, where it was combed into heaps and then spread by men with forks – a long, tiring job.

Threshing was hard and dirty work, although exciting for us children, who had the job of catching the mice. Wire netting was usually put round the corn stack and terriers were brought in to catch the rats, and there were usually a great many.

The arrival of the great steam engine was eagerly awaited. It would be drawing the drum and straw pitcher, quite a long procession, and very difficult to manipulate into position alongside the stack. Several men would be either walking or cycling behind, hoping for a day's casual work. The smell of the steam, and the throbbing of the engine, was something never forgotten. The corn sheaves were fed into the threshing drum one at a time by a man standing on the edge cutting the strings. The straw came, after the corn was beaten out, and was fed into the straw pitcher and went to other men waiting to build a straw stack.

Horses and tumbrels plied backwards and forwards to the barn with the full corn sacks, where men carried them to stack up in the dry. This was very hard work. Corn was measured by the 'coombe'; wheat 16 stones, barley 16 stones, beans 18 stones. It was very heavy work. The chaff was also saved, bagged up and carted inside, to be fed to the animals. Barley straw was put through a chaff cutter, also some hay. Cattle beet was grown to be shredded up and mixed with chaff and corn to feed the animals.

Growing sugar beet was a new thing, causing much hard work then. First, the beets were loosened from the soil by a horse-drawn lifter. Then they had to be pulled by hand, and knocked to shake off the soil and put in heaps. More men came along with beet hooks to top them and throw them into carts to take to heaps by the roadside. Later, when the lorry arrived, all the beet had to be thrown on with a hand fork, which took ages. Later an elevator was invented, which made loading easier. Imagine what a cold and miserable job it was, pulling and topping beet which, most of the time, would be covered in ice and snow.

Horse-drawn ploughs were a lovely sight. Most were pulled by two powerful horses. 'Suffolks' were strong, and many horsemen, very fond of their charges, would do their best to keep them in top condition, getting up very early to feed and groom them. An acre a day could be ploughed with a pair of horses and a one-furrow plough, meaning a lot of walking over rough ground.

As with all farm work with horses, much pride was taken – the furrows had to be very straight. Hedging and ditching were done in winter, a fire being lit to burn the bushes; this was warmth for the workers to sit by to eat their midday meal. 'Taters' were put into the ashes for a further treat.

The cowmen had a tedious job. Imagine a herd of 80 cows having to be milked by hand by these men twice a day, every day of the year, and then the milk had to be taken by bucket to the dairy.

LIFE ON THE FARM

I personally knew two of the farms very well, as they were in the Street. I was part of Rose Farm from the age of two. I spent much of my time with my aunt and uncle, at what is now Nors Cottage. My aunt was housekeeper for the Ling brothers up until 1964, after which she became owner and moved into the farm, after much renovation. This was what was known as a two-horse farm – about 50 acres. Charlie Ling was the horseman and did all the ploughing, harrowing and so on. Roger, his brother, milked the four cows twice a day. He fed the numerous chickens that ran free on the farm, and also on Hill Meadow up the lane.

Every building was full of stock; calves were reared on the surplus milk, then corn fed until they grew into huge beasts ready for sale. Likewise, pigs were fattened on the farm. Occasionally, one was taken to Hedley Rusted to be killed and the meat brought back to be prepared for use in the house. Most was salted down to last the winter (there were no fridges then). The meat was more fat than lean, but none was wasted.

There were several working horses that I remember, and all were treated very well. One bought by Charlie was called Smiler. He was a huge handsome bay, with a thick curly mane. However, Smiler was a problem, because if he didn't like someone, he promptly laid his ears back and bit them, and being a giant, his bite was not funny. He took an instant dislike to Roger Ling, and went for him one day, ripping the sleeve from his jacket and a chunk out of his arm. Smiler and I were good friends from the start, and I used to get him and his stable mate Bowler from the meadow in the morning. After his bate (breakfast), he would let me harness him, putting his great head down for me to put his collar on, which weighed nearly as much as I did.

The chaff house was the cats' favourite place to have their kittens; it was one of the first places I went to when I came to stay. The cats enjoyed the freedom of the house. When the Ling brothers ate, it was always on the old kitchen table, with a newspaper 'tablecloth'. Up to five cats sat on the table round their plates and all got a share of their food, waiting their turn patiently. An old-fashioned open fire was the only heat in the house, and over this, on a hook, was a huge iron kettle; tea was made in an enamel teapot and left on the hob all day, winter and summer. The old boys would come in and drink from its spout. A boiler also hung from the hook, the hot water from which was used to heat water for the calves' milk. All water was brought in, either from a pump or from the pond. The only light was from candles. My aunt cooked potatoes for the brothers, and baked huge shortcakes and rusks, but their main diet was salt pork, bread and cheese.

There were four meadows then. The one we call Hill Meadow was full of beautiful wild flowers, including three kinds of orchid, cowslips, primroses and violets. All produced mushrooms in the late summer. The dairy was on the cool end of the house. It had wooden slatted windows and a brick floor, with a drain going through the middle. A few people bought milk at the door, bringing their jugs or cans to be filled. The rest was put into shallow pans, left for a day; then the cream was taken off with a 'flete' – a kind of strainer – and put aside to make butter. This was done once or twice a week and the butter sold to the shop or directly to local people. The skimmed milk was fed to the animals. The salt pork was stored in the dairy, as were the eggs, after washing; they were collected each week.

There were lovely apples and plums growing in the orchard. Apples were stored on the floor of a bedroom, and lasted all winter.

One of the things I liked to see was when the horses came in from their hard day's work; they were allowed to wade into the horse pond for a long drink, and to cool their legs. The cows also enjoyed this.

Street Farm was a fine old-fashioned place where many men worked, including Dido Pearce, Cyril Riches, Will Flatt, Clifford Knowles and Harsent Runnacles. There were six or eight horses there, and at harvest time it was a wonderful sight to see these coming from St James Road and up the Street, with their wagons full of sheaves. Some even came on their own, they knew the way so well. They went into the stackyard, through the front gate, were unloaded, and then led off back down the Spong to be reloaded. Cliff Knowles had a very nasty experience when he was ploughing with a pair of horses during the war. A plane from Metfield airfield crash-landed, killing both animals. This was a great shock for him; he loved his horses.

Gurney (Duck) Godbold owned Street Farm, where he lived from the late 1930s with his wife May. He owned a threshing tackle, which was hired out to the surrounding farms. Claude and Charlie Barley and their fathers used to travel with the engine.

Tom Godbold lived at the Willows and another brother Ernie was at Office Farm. Tom had many workers and a large milking herd. The corn stacks at the Willows were a work of art; rows of identical round shapes, all beautifully thatched, and decorated with corn dollies. Tom's wife Laura was a teacher at Metfield. The Godbold brothers supplied the horses to pull the snow plough in winter; another lovely sight.

A TIME OF CHANGE

Many houses were demolished in the 1930s. Several stood around Skinners Green, including two beside St John's Cottage and others down Grove Lane, past the cemetery. There were two on the left, opposite Hillside on the Withersdale Road, two more on the lane leading to Valley Farm and more near Metfield Garage. In the 1960s, Miss

Edith Squire, with her own hands, demolished two houses, which stood behind the Firs, leaving part of one as a garage for herself. This earned her a page in the local paper, together with a photo.

Between 1934 and 1938, the first three pairs of council houses were built, about the same time as the 'new' Vicarage, which came about on the bottom of Brick Kiln field. Soon after the war, several prefabs were erected, where Field Close is now. These were the wonder of that time, arriving in sections on large lorries. They had fitted kitchens, with an electric cooker and fridge. They also had a bathroom, an unheard-of luxury then. The people who moved into these bungalows were the envy of the village.

No more council houses were built until the 1960s, when land was bought from Town Farm. Then the bungalows began to appear along Skinner's Green, nine in all. This land was bought from Hedley Rusted, and had previously been a meadow, occupied by pigs and their sties. Gradually all the spare bits of land were sold and built on, including St John's Meadow.

The Methodist Chapel, built about 150 years ago, was very well attended in the early years. It also had a good Sunday School. Alterations carried out around 1970 made room for a meeting room on the back, with a kitchen and toilet added. St John's Church is a fine building, about 600 years old. Like many others, it used to be full most Sundays; the choir had more members than the congregation does today. At that time, the churchwardens were George Runnacles, Tom Godbold, Duck Godbold and Jack Pretty.

Marjorie Edgcombe has been organist for both church and chapel for around 55 years.

George Harper and his wife Violet did many duties for the church for more than 40 years. These included church cleaning, clock winding, churchyard maintenance and ringing the three bells. They were members of the Parochial Church Council. It must be said that everything was done the hard way then. The oil lamps had to be filled and trimmed, the coal or oil heaters maintained and the brasses polished. All the cleaning was done with a broom, brush and dustpan; the pay was poor. The church was always immaculate. Sadly, George died suddenly in 1980. Violet couldn't cope on her own, so now there is a rota for cleaning and flower arranging.

THE VILLAGE AT WAR

The war years in Metfield were similar to those in most villages. I was nine years old when war started. Evacuees were sent to our village, and most houses took in one or more. My uncle failed his medical test for the forces so, like many others, he joined the Home Guard. I think the locals enjoyed this; it gave them confidence and they felt they were 'doing their bit'. The Home Guard had a headquarters hut on Squire's meadow, where some of them spent each night. Concrete 'pillboxes' were built, several in each village, at vantage points where there were clear views over the countryside. Members of the Home Guard also manned the church tower to watch for invaders. My uncle, like many others, built an air-raid shelter in the orchard. He dug a square pit about six feet deep and cut steps down to it. Stout wood was laid across the top, then sheets of galvanised iron which were covered with turf. Inside, he put seats, candles and matches for night use. Mercifully, the shelter was never really needed. The Germans in their planes took pleasure in coming in very low in daylight, strafing villages with machine gun bullets. Luckily no one was hurt, but many roof tiles were damaged.

A bomb did drop at the bottom of Jubilee Meadow; it made a crater there, bounced over Brick Kiln Cottages (there were two of them then) and exploded in the field beside what was then the Vicarage. It almost demolished a lovely house opposite, in which was a bedridden man who escaped with minor injuries. His wife, who was out shopping, returned to find her home in ruins. Much damage was also done to other houses nearby.

Metfield airfield was built during 1940. The sleepy village suddenly came alive as dozens of gravel lorries roared through and hundreds of Irish labourers arrived. The men lived in wooden buildings on Fressingfield Road. Farms and houses were demolished, fields and trees vanished under concrete; it was never to be the same again. Soon there was the roar of aircraft engines, first the Thunderbolt fighters – noisy things – then the more majestic Liberator bombers. It was sometime during this period that the terrible bomb dump explosion occurred, claiming the lives of several American servicemen. Although damage was done in the village – doors were blown off and windows were broken – the main wave of the explosion went towards Halesworth, thus saving more damage and possible loss of life.

METFIELD CHARACTERS

There were some wonderful old characters in the village, all well-known locals, in fact many were related. It was said that one had to live here for at least 20 years to become a native. Charlie and Lena Denmark lived in the cottage adjoining Johnny Reilly and Dick and Laura West at the top of the Street. Both were a bit deaf and argued continually but were very devoted and lived to celebrate their diamond wedding anniversary. Mrs West was a staunch churchgoer, being on the Parochial Church Council and helping with all church functions. Dick enjoyed gardening and meeting his cronies at the pub for a yarn and a pint. Emma Rusted, another member of the local family, lived to a great age; she lived on the corner. Next to her at the Forge was 'young' Ambrose Clutterham (Honey) and his wife; he moved into Red House when his father died. The Bell House was a private school in the early days, the Misses Hadingham living there.

Honeymoon Row was a row of five assorted cottages, before the 'renovations'. People were always moving in and out. Harsent and Daisy Runnacles, and Joan, lived for many years in number two; Jack and Dora Pipe in number one. On the other end was Rose Luke, her brother having died early on. Rosie was a special village lady, a spinster, who rode her high stepper bike until well into her nineties, her back as straight as a dart. She attended church regularly, falling in love with each of the vicars in turn. She lived to over 100 years old.

Lib Riches was landlady of the old Duke William for many years, and also took on the newly built Duke. She was assisted by Charlie Barley, a lovely old boy, who lived with his parents next to the Old Duke. Next was Lizzie Larter, a widow who had a daughter Ivy. Her brother 'Gunner' Wolner, an old soldier, lived with her.

Then there was Savage's shop. Next at the Firs resided Willy Squire and Annie, his wife. I can remember a farmer named Bolton at Street Farm. Gurney Godbold married May Hadingham in the late 1930s and took over the farm. The Ling brothers farmed what is now Rose Farm for many years. A succession of people lived at Nook Cottage, which was thatched in the old days. The last, longer living lady was Elsie Pfister; her husband Teddy died in the 1960s. At Guildhall Cottage lived George Runnacles with Margaret, for all their married life. They were a lovely couple with many talents. After working in Yorkshire, where he met his future wife, George worked for the Godbolds until his retirement. They both gave devoted service to church work, being on the Parochial Church Council and in the choir. George was clerk to the Parish Council for many years, and was very clever at drawing up plans for buildings.

Mrs Harper's parents, Mrs and Mr David Warne, resided round Skinners Green, as did Mr and Mrs Buggs, Geoff's grandparents, and several other families. A little old lady nicknamed 'six foot' lived in the small house adjoining St John's Cottage, while Miss Watkiss was in the main house; she kept poultry. Ralph and Mrs Eastaugh were tenants at Town Farm with their children Brian, Derek and Pat. A herd of cows grazed where Town Farm Close now is. Billy and Celia Whatling lived at Homestead.

Coming back to the Street, Church Cottage was at one time the vicarage, but later the home of a school teacher. The headmistress always lived in the schoolhouse, which was formerly the village poorhouse. Elmore Cottage was the home of John and Laura Elmore for all their married life. John, a builder by trade, was standing on the ridge of Metfield Church, doing repairs, when he was in his eighties. He had the first motorcycle in the village and took Laura out in his wicker basket sidecar. He also had an early motorcar, a Ford Model T, in which he did hire work for the locals. His nephew and partner in business, Les Davy and Eva, were next door.

What is now Half Moon Cottage was the home of two real characters. In the first house was Liza Wolner, grandmother of Thelma Rayner. An old man, Orlando, lived with her until his passing. Next door was a Mrs Larter, whose grandson Rowley lived with her. She looked the same all the time I knew her. She had a very wrinkled face and always wore a cap. These two seemed to stand in their doorways most of the day, watching the comings and goings. Mr Clutterham senior, at Red House; then Teddy Poppy, Mrs Watson and Harold Edgecombe, her foster son. George and Vi Harper lived in their cottage all their married life; Vi was born up the top of Christmas Lane, with the rest of her family. Several farms and cottages were up there; one housed a family with thirteen children. It was quite a little community, up until the airfield appeared. All used to walk to school, meeting up with the Knowles children, who lived in a house which I believe burned down, where now is Metfield Garage. Harry Shipton came home after serving in the Second World War, to make the garage as it is now. Hillside was a 'three dweller'. An Oxborough lived in one, and also 'Jumbo' Vincent.

The Fishers farmed Oak Hill. Up the lane at Rookery Farm lived some Flatts, before the last lot, two ladies and a man, who pushed a hand cart to the Street, from which he sold milk. After their demise came Charlie and May Flatt with their son Lennie, really the last of the old type of farmer. May rarely left the place; she dressed in long clothes, covered by a sack mantle. Her daily outing was collecting eggs from the stacks and the surrounding buildings. If she saw anyone walking up the lane, she quickly disappeared indoors. Charlie walked up to the village, or occasionally went to market with Lennie. It was a great day for them when they bought a generator and had electricity for the first time.

THE PLEASURES OF LIFE

Mains electricity was brought into Metfield after the Second World War, I think the early 1950s. Likewise, the water was laid on to most houses around this time. Previously, people had pumps in their gardens, or fetched water in buckets from the nearest pond. Everyone had water butts that caught the rainwater from the roofs; this was used for washing clothes and so on. Main sewer works were put through the village about 1970.

The allotments were a hive of activity, there being about 18 plots, all occupied and worked with pride. Also this was a meeting place, where leisure time was spent, and somewhere to get out of the way of the missus. Sometimes more time was spent yarning than working. Having said this, some wonderful fruit, vegetables and flowers were grown, amid great competition and not a little jealousy. A few pigs were even kept on the bottom allotment. I spent happy evenings with my uncle, helping to dig potatoes and listening to the 'old boys'.

A flower show was held every year on the Jubilee Meadow, with many fine entries by the men, prepared over previous weeks. The women entered competitions for flowers, cooking and needlework. There was fancy dress for children and sports for all ages. It was the event of the year.

The village hall, built around 1930, was well used. There were whist drives, social evenings and regular dances held there. All the villagers enjoyed the different functions then; the people were united. Most were on very low wages but were content and friendly, enjoying the small pleasures of life in their village.

ABOUT THE AUTHOR

Evelyn Whiting was born in Stradbroke, Suffolk on 26 August 1929, but it was to the village of Metfield that she gave her heart when, from the age of three, she was regularly brought over to stay with her aunt and uncle – Lesley and Eva Davey. Lesley was a builder and Eva acted as housekeeper to the Ling brothers, who lived in Rose Farm in the centre of Metfield. This was to be the scene of Evelyn's happiest childhood memories, and the beginning of her lifelong devotion to all animals – particularly the farm horses.

Evelyn and her husband Russell (a 'horseman', naturally) later set up home in Metfield with their two children, becoming immersed in village life and particularly the life of the church, to which they gave many loyal hours. However, horses remained their first love, and in later years they were frequently to be seen bowling along (dressed for the part) in their brightly turned-out pony and trap.

Evelyn died on 18 November 2004 and is buried in Metfield cemetery.

ANOTHER METFIELD BOOK

**Metfield Parish and Poor
in the Late Eighteenth Century** by Victor Peskett

What was life like for the rural poor in 18th century England? Just as new agricultural technology was replacing farm workers with machines, medical advances were improving life expectancy. The result in rural Suffolk was a scarcity of employment that left many without the means to support their families. In a fascinating glimpse into community action at a local level, Victor Peskett reveals in this book the workings of the Guardians of the Poor in Metfield, Suffolk, a village committee with powers to levy a charge on the community and dispense funds to support the poor, according to their needs and their means.

Peskett's painstaking research into the minutes of the Guardians' meetings has uncovered not the dry transactions of a local administrative committee, but an illumination of the past two short centuries ago. We come to know the characters that emerge from the old vellum-bound, handwritten record – their clothes, their few possessions, their daily transactions and their squabbles but, most of all, their urgent and basic needs at a time when progress seemed to be leaving them behind.

**Available from Metfield Church and as an ebook and
in print from all good online retailers.**

www.ingramcontent.com/pod-product-compliance
Lightning Source LLC
Chambersburg PA
CBHW070254290526
45789CB00004B/1847